Out of the Wilderness

Out of the Wilderness

Leah Johns

RESOURCE *Publications* · Eugene, Oregon

OUT OF THE WILDERNESS

Copyright © 2021 Leah Johns. All rights reserved. Except for brief quotations in critical publications or reviews, no part of this book may be reproduced in any manner without prior written permission from the publisher. Write: Permissions, Wipf and Stock Publishers, 199 W. 8th Ave., Suite 3, Eugene, OR 97401.

Resource Publications
An Imprint of Wipf and Stock Publishers
199 W. 8th Ave., Suite 3
Eugene, OR 97401

www.wipfandstock.com

PAPERBACK ISBN: 978-1-6667-1138-7
HARDCOVER ISBN: 978-1-6667-1139-4
EBOOK ISBN: 978-1-6667-1140-0

JULY 6, 2021

Scripture taken from The Message. Copyright © 1993, 1994, 1995, 1996, 2000, 2001, 2002. Used by permission of NavPress Publishing Group.

To the lost and broken,
There is joy in heaven when one lost sheep is found.
Jesus came to save and restore the broken.
He came to set us free.

Contents

The Reason | xi

The Child

Hush ... Please | 3
Trembling | 4
Jesus Loves Me | 5
Secure | 6
I'm Special | 7
My Own Room | 8
Stay Home | 9
Smothered | 10
Not So Hard | 11

Marriage

Where's My Place? | 15
At Last | 16
Values Instilled | 17
Cherish | 18
Duplicity | 19
Bigger | 21
His Fix | 22
God Planned | 23
Which Is It? | 24

Divorce

Up to You | 27
She Calls Again | 29
His Needs | 30
Filed | 31
Really | 32
Replacement | 33

Together, But Not

Again | 37
Empowered by Me | 38
His Compliment | 39
Where Are You? | 40
Seventy—Three Calls | 41
Alibi | 42
My Case | 43
Counsel for Him | 44
Secrets | 46
Elusive | 47

Broken

Lost | 51
Crazy | 52
Shame | 53
The Choice | 54
Normal | 55

Into the Light

Fenced | 59
Relative | 60
To Church | 61
Help | 62

Loyalty | 64
I Pray | 65

Hope

No Veil | 69
Yielded | 70
Sunrise | 71
Learn | 72
Released | 73
Armed | 74
Parallel Lives | 75
Forever | 76

Future

Eyes Open | 79
Advice | 80
Speculate | 81
Forgive | 82

Challenging

Challenging | 85
Harder Than I Thought | 86
Afterthoughts | 87
Hereafter | 88
How? | 89
Promise | 90
No Regrets | 92

Next

My Parents | 95
R & R | 96
Community | 97

Maturity | 99
Today | 100
History | 101
Why So Long? | 102
Take Heart | 104
Another Today | 105
Next | 106
Your Neighbor | 107

Final Thoughts | 109

BIBLIOGRAPHY | 111

The Reason

WE LEARN FROM OUR EXPERIENCES, especially during our formative years. Growing up in a critical, controlling environment does not foster confidence and optimism. What if anxiety and low esteem are dominant factors in our lives? What if as we grow and become adults, we choose and perpetuate relationships that suborn what has become poverty of spirit? What if we feel valued not for who we are, but for what we accomplish, the work we do, and the enabling of others? Will feelings of inadequacy always be there to haunt and undermine? What happens if the load is too heavy? What happens when a self destructive path is chosen? Can there be hope? Can one be redeemed and worthy? We have it on good authority, that there is hope and much more. There is the promise of an abundant life waiting for our embrace.

> Our firm decision is to work from this focused center: One man died for everyone. That puts everyone in the same boat. He included everyone in His death so that everyone could be included in His life, a resurrection life, a far better life than people ever lived on their own.
> (2 Cor 5:14–15, MSG)

On a night not so long ago, I was exhausted, but could not sleep. I was ashamed and repentant, but could not find peace. My thoughts chased each other through the night never finding resolution. I finally rested, then slept, when I decided to write this story. I did not know where to begin, but within a few days, words and lines began to come to me. This collection of poems is the result.

The Child

*Leave the children alone, don't prevent them from coming to Me.
God's kingdom is made up of people like them.*

—MATTHEW 19:14, NKJV

Hush . . . Please

Hush little baby. Don't say a word.
Daddy's gonna buy you a mockingbird.
If that mockingbird don't sing,
Daddy's gonna buy you a diamond ring.[1]

Eyes open wide.
No more songs in my head.
Shouts in my ears,
Screams in my head,
Relaxed to rigid,
Rigid to trembling,
Lying to standing.
The crib rail is up.
I can't run away.
"No, 'top! Pease 'top!"
No one stops. No one hears.
"No 'top! Pease 'top!"
No one stops. No one hears.
Shouts in my ears,
Screams in my head.
Standing to crouching,
Trembling in my bed.
No escape.

---

1. "Hush Little Baby." Traditional lullaby thought to have been written in the Southern United States. Author and date of origin are unknown.

Trembling

"Little girl,
Raise your head."
The voice, I guess, was in my head.
"I cannot look," I said.

Shouts, maybe hits.
Shouts, sometimes hits.

"Take your clothes.
Get out," she says.
"I built this house.
I'll stay," he says.

Shouts, Shouts, Shouts

"Little girl, raise your head."
The voice again.
"Does no one care for me?" I asked.
There are no tears for me to shed.
Just a trembling body curled in bed.

Jesus Loves Me

Jesus,
My Creator, my Savior, my Advocate.
More than I can grasp.
More than I can comprehend.
So simple even a child can understand.

We sang "Just As I Am" in that little country church.
Verses one, two, and four.
Whosoever will may come.
I asked, "Can I go?"
Alone, age five, I walked down the aisle,
And gave my heart to Jesus.

Secure

So is a five year old really saved?
Years later I wondered,
So unworthy I felt.
So much time on my knees to repent.
"Yes," the revival preacher said.
"A child with the interest, the intellect,
The instruction can certainly make that decision."

And so saved at five, a believer I became,
Taught by teachers in Sunday School,
Given an anchor through the storms.
My hold was weak, but His hold was strong.
So often close to insanity.
My hold was weak, but His hold was strong.

I'm Special

They record attendance at my church.
Perfect attendance all year!
A pin for me and a gold star each Sunday.
Then another, another; I don't miss.
They talk about Jesus, His stories, and more.

I learned all the books of the *Bible*.
Recited them out loud,
Just a little help with one or two.
A special gift for me, a new *Bible*!
My teacher's name and mine,
Written under "Belongs To".

My Own Room

I have my own room,
But I don't.

Used to be a porch,
Enclosed now for me.
My desk, my bed,
My mother sleeping next to me.

Why does she stay?
Why won't she go?
I'm not afraid.
Monsters in this house, but not under my bed.

Daddy calls. "Come in here," he says.
Daddy calls. She ignores him again.

Why doesn't she go?
He wants her in his bed.
Why doesn't she go?
I'm not afraid of the dark.

Stay Home

If I stay home,
Maybe I'll bring peace.
If I stay home,
Maybe they won't fight.

I stay home.
Maybe I can mediate.
Really?
Me? A little girl.
I thought so then.
Stay home.
Fear grips me again.

Stay home.
I'm not afraid of the dark.
I'm afraid of them.

Smothered

Her advice,
Her admonitions,
Her warnings,
Her guilt.

Why won't my mother give me room?
Why does she invade my space?
Over my shoulder always looking,
Advising, correcting.
What am I doing wrong?

I have chores at home and I have a job.
I study; I'm an honor student.
I go to church.
I love the Lord.
Give me some space.

I need to breathe.

Not So Hard

So off to college
"Why so far?" my mother asked.
"The scholarship is there," I answered,
"Applied and got it myself."

Off to college,
The binding is broken.
No friends from home,
I am on my own.
Tentative, yet eager,
I can do this, I know.

"The worst day of my life," my mother said.
I went home for summers and such,
But never again within her clutch.

Marriage

And the Lord God said, "It is not good that man should be alone; I will make him a helper comparable to him."

—GENESIS 2:18, NKJV

Where's My Place?

I can't seem to find it.
A husband, a family,
Don't seem in my reach.

I visited back home.
My parents I see and
Aunts, uncles, the whole family.

Also back to the church of my childhood and youth;
A charter member I'm proud to recall.
"Still single?" they asked.
"Why isn't a nice girl like you already married?"

At Last

I think it's love.
It feels that way to me.
I like him.
He certainly likes me.

Home to each family we go.
Mine likes him and his likes me.
Interests in common,
Values we share,
A way of life that seems compatible.

A small concern for me is age.
I'm a little older than he.
So one day I ask,
"When you think of me,
Is it a girl or a woman that you see?"
"I think of you as a lady," he says.
His answer is all the assurance I need.

I think it's love.

Values Instilled

His home was chaotic.
Mine was too.
Yelling and anger and fighting most days.

His home was permissive.
Those kids did no wrong.
No work for them either.
Their momma would do it.

Mine was restrictive,
Guilt zealously honed.
Plenty of work for all of us.
No real innocence for anyone.

Cherish

To love and to cherish;
Isn't that what he vowed?

His needs are abundant,
Conveyed to me without any doubt.

"I have needs too," I try to explain.
"Don't make excuses or change the subject."
He's told me before.

To love and to cherish,
Doesn't that include me?
His answer so blunt, so hard to take in,
"You're not that kind of woman to me."

I thought I was a lady,
To love, honor, and protect.
But now as my husband,
This view he does not reflect.

Duplicity

He does what he wants, regardless of me.
If I don't agree, that's too bad for me.
What he wants, likes, and needs,
That's his priority.
If my feelings are hurt, it's not his concern.
If his focus is always on another, so what?
He's a friendly guy.

Help around the house? He wasn't raised for that.
He has work, community clubs, and golf.
Don't forget church; he's active there.

So in an effort for peace, I think I can do it all.
Taking care of the children is my priority.
Be involved in church, the community too.
Keep house, do the shopping,
Fix the meals, run the errands.
Feels kind of like Cinderella to me.

Don't forget my job.
I stayed home a few years when the children were small.
But I think my work is important too.

He said, "Stay home if you want."
I needed to get out.
The children and I had the same hours.
So working, a possibility, became our reality.
People called me a gifted teacher.
That affirmation was important to me.

He does what he wants regardless of me.
If I don't agree, it's still too bad for me.
What he wants and likes, his needs are the priority.
I pull away, but he pulls me back.
His words say, "I love you."
His actions scream, "Need."
His message to me? Double, but clear.

Bigger

More to love?
He doesn't think so.
Two or three pounds add up each year.

Lose some weight.
I try—every plan, every program.
There are many.

It's a choice.
Easy for some; not so for many.
Not anyone's choice, really.

Am I that bad?
Insults come in many forms.

His Fix

Don't be angry.
Don't be stubborn.
Get over it. Life goes on.

Sex makes everything right.
Don't you see?

God Planned

Sex, created by God.
For procreation,
For love,
Within marriage, for pleasure.
That was my desire.

Haunted by sin.
Haunted by memories.
The devil's fiery darts.

Which Is It?

He loves me.
He loves me not.

If love, why not expressed?
Why no kindnesses large or small?
Why no tokens for memories sake?
Why no surprises to delight?
Why no help to ease the strain?

He loves me not.

Divorce

And I say to you, whoever divorces his wife except for sexual immorality . . .

—MATTHEW 19:9A, NKJV

Up to You

"I'll get a divorce," he tells me again.
Emboldened by what, I don't know.
"Go ahead," I tell him, " the choice is yours.
We'll need support, the girls and I."

"Support from me? You gotta be kidding.
I have standards to keep in my line of work.
People who see me know that's true.
Places to go, things to do.
You'll have to get by.
I can spare a little,
But most of it will be up to you."

"So what do I do?" I ask myself.
A teacher's salary doesn't go far.
We've moved so often for his new jobs,
I've had no chance to get ahead.

"So what do I do?" I ask myself.
My nerves are a mess.
I cannot think.
I need to be steady,
To help myself.
That bottle in the house I found,
It gave me warmth, a brief escape.
I'll try that again.
"Hello, my friend." Vodka again.

She Calls Again

Another call.
So many.
"Who is this? " I ask.
His answer, "The guys; it's sports and golf."

My bathroom,
Our bathroom,
Towels used,
Hung up wrong.

Whose jewelry? Left on the tub.
Left in our bathroom, but not mine.

His Needs

He says I need to be counseled again.
He says he'll go, but not with me.
"I'll find my own," he says.
He said that he went, was counseled,
And is finished.
Was told he had no further need;
He's good to go.

"I'll be gone this week-end," he tells me.
He gives me his list of needs going forward:
Go to work.
Take care of the house.
A little more cooking would be very nice.
Accompany him on occasions as needed.
After all, I must understand.
He has standards to keep.
So now, what do I do?

"Hello again, Vodka, my old friend."

Filed

"Divorce,
I filed today,"
I told him.
"No lawyers," he says.
"We can work it out."

The house sitter found pornography on our computer.
"Not mine," he says, "must be yours or our daughter's."
Technical analysis showed it too,
Abundant and frequently accessed.
"No, not mine," he denies again.
"I never look at porn."
Denied, more loudly denied.
Does he think volume equals truth?

Really

His conclusion:
She really divorced me.
I didn't think she had it in her.

I gave her the house.
Couldn't let it go to trial.
Too many details would come out.
I have standards to keep in my line of work.
People who see me know that's true.
Places to go; things to do.

This condo is fine.
Who needs a house?
I surely won't miss her.
But I do miss my stuff,
Her cooking, her cleaning, and some basic needs.

I can replace her; I'm sure that I can.
Maybe someone younger this time.

Replacement

His perspective:
It's harder than I thought.
I've tried a few, more than a couple,
But they don't really quite fit in.

The places I go, the people I see.
I thought her replacement would be pretty easy.
But these others don't seem to do it for me.
I miss her listening, her meals, now her house.
I can't take these others to church with me.

So the solution is clear; now I get it.
I'll get her back and also my stuff.
My home, her family, my respectability.
I can change; I can get her to agree.
I can change, if she'll only help me.

Together, But Not

The Lord is near to those who have a broken heart, and saves such as have a contrite spirit.

PSALM 34:18, NKJV

Again

Take him back, I ponder.
Reconcile, I wonder.
Having my family together again.
No more holidays split between.
Not so hard to make ends meet.

"I've really changed," he tells me again.
"I'll do better;
I promise I will.
I get so confused.
I just need your help."

Empowered by Me

Where it started, I'm not sure.
A strong woman I was thought to be.
From humble beginnings with no doubt,
But taught to work. I learned well.
Work hard, pray hard.
It will all work out.

I still can't see where the turn started.
There were choices made, but not for me.
Compliments given, but not to me.
Anger, resentment masked my pain.
Hurt at what I thought life would be.
Little by little, my confidence eroded.

When it just got so hard I had to escape,
My good friend, Vodka, provided the gate.
 Caring to carefree, stressed to relaxed;
That's how I gave him empowerment.

His Compliment

"I have an ache," he says,
"You can make it go away.
It always goes away with you."
He tells me, "You are the best."

Is this a compliment? I wonder.
Does he think this turns me on?

"After sex with you," he says,
"I turn right over and
I sleep so well."

I sigh, ya think?
He doesn't even turn over,
Before he's snoring.

Where Are You?

It's late,
Long after work.
It's night.
I text, "Are you okay?"

Morning—Not home.
Directions to an address miles away.
An iPad search he didn't think I'd see.
"Who is she?" I ask.
His answer, "A friend,
Only a friend, not seen in years.
I didn't go there; I just didn't come here."

I searched our account—thirteen calls to her this month.
He maintained only a phone friend he had never seen.
There had been no drinking for a long time.
But again Vodka beckoned and I answered the call.

Seventy—Three Calls

He explains,
"I've stopped talking to her.
She was just a friend.
I explained to her that it made you upset.
Let's get on with our lives, you and me.
She understood,
And so I have stopped.
Check our phone account.
No calls to her at all this month."
So I checked,
And he was right.
But I've gotten a bit savvy.
So I went back six months,
To when they started.
Seventy-three calls between the two.
"A judge won't buy it," I tell him.
My heart filled with fear again.
"But I'm telling you straight," was his reply.
"We can work this out.
Believe me please. I don't even know how she looks.
Haven't seen her in years."

Alibi

His grumbling, impatience,
Abruptness I think I comprehend.
His mind on another,
Three weekends away, without any notice.
I can't buy his alibi.
Says he doesn't know what she looks like.
That's a lie too.
She is his Facebook friend and she likes to post.
I bring it up, and voila, that Facebook page disappears.

How do I go on?
Can anyone fathom how I feel?
We just moved.
No friends for confiding or to recommend an attorney.
He doesn't want a divorce.
He maintains she was only a friend.
A bit excessive, he did admit.
But friendship only, he sticks to his script.
I don't believe him, but I try.
"Let's take a class on marriage," he suggests.
"Our new church offers one."
So off we go, another try.
Maybe we'll find God's perspective.
Neither of us had seen that in our homes growing up.

My Case

In the door,
Long drive home.

Bed is made.
Not like I make it.
Hair on the sheets,
Not mine, not his.

I write it all down.
Every word is an affront.
My senses are numb.

I find counsel.
This is no way to live.
An attorney is needed.
I have decided.
I've made my case.

"The church has counselors," he says,
"I'll make an appointment and go."

Counsel for Him

Counselor told him,
"Be thankful for your wife."

Better life,
Think we'll be okay.

Time with family,
Blessed.

No compassion,
No passion,
But I can live like this.
Remind him of occasions.
Remind him of events.

Thankful.
No arguments.
I have time.
I can take care of all this.

He criticizes,
He complains,
At least not about me.
Can he listen a little?
Must he always have an iPhone or iPad in his hand?
"I hear you," he says.
"How can he ?" I wonder,
"When nothing I say has any effect."

Secrets

Asleep on the sofa as I try to talk.
No plans except the ones I've made.
My perfunctory roll is clear.
Life can be hard,
Comes fast sometimes.

Hard to adjust with someone
Who takes, but does not give.
Who judges, but does not affirm.
Who locks his phone, his email account too.
Yet,
Who carelessly fails to delete an often visited site.
Who feigns ignorance at what I've found.
Then finally concedes, "We can agree to disagree on if it is pornography."

Days of history he failed to clear.
No words, no volume can validate.
His volume does not equal truth.
Angry, distracted, his secrets abound.

Elusive

Organized and thorough,
Don't procrastinate, don't waste time.
Make a list, stay focused.
Be productive each day.

A bit out of kilter,
I can't quite explain it.
I am not anxious;
I know better than that.

Something within me,
Not settled, not balanced.
Aha! Shocked, dismayed,
Comprehension sinks into my being.

Understanding the puzzle I live.
Seeking harmony in the company of one,
Gratified by those he intimately views.
Anger and distraction are his too.

Broken

Therefore He is also able to save to the uttermost those who come to God through Him, since He always lives to make intercession for them.

—HEBREWS 7:25, NKJV

Lost

Where am I going?
I do not know.
Walking, walking, walking.

Where am I?
I do not know.
"Can we call someone for you?" they ask.
"Please, no," I answer them.
"We must; you cannot be here alone."
Despite my protests,
He came for me and so they left.

No peace for me with him.

Crazy

I hear him talking to my child on the phone.
"She's crazy,
Running in the woods.
Called me to get her.
Out of her mind."

I want to stay away,
But I must go home.
No peace here.
No peace there.
No peace for me anywhere.

Shame

Again.
How could I?

Each day,
"More like You," I pray.
Each day,
"Lead me by Your Spirit."
Each day,
"Try me; know my thoughts,
If there are any grievous ways, restore me."
Each day,
"Show me my hidden faults."
Each day,
"Keep me from presumptuous sin."

I pray.
I am thankful.
I am humble before Him.

How could I?
Again.

The Choice

Go on;
Pretend I did not see.
Pretend there's no effect on me.
Pretend I think he's what he seems.
Pretend I won't succumb again.

My life, one pretense after another;
If I try hard enough, if I work hard enough . . .
I can fill the gap.
I know I can . . . but
Not a gap, but an abyss.
Not enough for him and me.
Finally I see.

I must save me.

Normal

Chastened,
Forgiven,
Back to normal he thinks.

Deja vu
The shape I was in,
Won't make it again.

No confrontation,
No sudden change.
No words from him.
He thinks I'll cave.

No choice for me.
Can't try again.
Futility would win again.

Not strong enough for one more try.
It is on Him I must rely.

Into the Light

The fear of the Lord is the beginning of wisdom, and the knowledge of the Holy One is understanding.

—PROVERBS 9:10, NKJV

Fenced

Fenced by his choices.
Leave.
She knows too much.
People will know.
Too much to lose.

Stay.
A thin facade.
Yet a facade.

Change.
No longer a choice?
Hardened by time?

He looks, but does not see.
He listens, but does not hear.

Relative

Anger, not said in words.
Passive aggressive now his watchword.

When I went down,
He seemed lifted up.
How could that be?
The answer too clear.
Need is not love.
That's what he had for me.
Duplicity was his game.
So often I was taken in.

His scapegoat still present,
But not as before.
Transformed, but how?
He does not know.

He wants it like it was before. So superior he could be.
At least he wasn't as bad as me.

To Church

He goes to church.
He seldom misses.
He sings, he prays,
He even takes notes.
Doesn't that count?

God judges the heart.
God knows the motive.
What's for him?
Not mine to say; it is mine to pray.

How many chances?
God draws each soul near.
How many chances? Only God knows.

How many chances?
Before his heart hardens?
Break him with whatever it takes.
Bring him to repentance is my plea.
May he decide before eternity.

Help

Counselors for marriage, alcohol, depression,
I have been to many.
Some said leave him; some said meditate.
Many suggestions of books for me to read.

They listened at first; soon I listened to them.
These counselors had struggles, trials, and needs.
The role reversal never took long.

My children said to keep looking or
Find a friend in whom to confide.
But not to them, after all, he is their dad.
Their point was well taken.
I could not deny it.

I needed a friend in whom to confide.
I had two or three along the way.
But never one who seemed to stay.
Friends for socializing and eating out.
But not one with whom to share my hurt and my doubt.
So I went on, trying to stand strong.
Always willing and called on to help others.
I've tried over and over to make a life with him.
It's good for a while, but his needs override.
I gradually start the decline.

I don't see it coming.
By now I should have learned.
Life with him spreads me pretty thin.
And I end up drinking again.

Loyalty

All these years of marriage,
All the double messages of love.
What he needed was an outlet.
His anger and shame projected to me.

I made a home, gave respectability.
His house of cards, flimsy at best.
My determination to make it work, never enough.
My hope in him, my thoughts askew.

There wasn't enough of me to keep going.
My fragile hopes were misplaced.
My position has changed.
No more trying to walk beside him as wife.
Striving to please him, never a reality.
The heart space for compassion and love for his wife,
Long displaced by lust and love for himself.

He could manage briefly to be a good husband.
But only briefly,
Because his loyalty was never to me.

I Pray

Salvation is a gift to accept or reject,
Bought at a price.
Paid for with blood.
On a cross, so cruel I can hardly grasp it.

Each must work out his own salvation,
The Apostle Paul teaches.
God works both to will and to do,
For His good pleasure.

So each day I pray for him.
Please God, "Let him have eyes to see.
Let him have ears to hear
Let him know your promises are real."

God calls us all, but forces none.
There is no sin too grave to forgive.
People can be fooled, but God cannot.
His requirements simple and profound:
You must repent and change.

Hope

For I know the thoughts that I think toward you, says the Lord, thoughts of peace and not of evil, to give you a future and a hope.

—JEREMIAH 29:11, NKJV

No Veil

From the depths,
The glimmer of hope,
The light of truth,
The beacon of promises.

Always there.
The veil removed.
New life embraced.

Yielded

Yielded and mended is my desire.
My understanding and reasoning long delayed.
A smart one like me, why so long to figure it out?
Can't see the future,
Don't understand what is true.
Can His promises really include me too?
Loved by others, so they said.
But love not shown, not expressed,
Is not love, I now realize.

Yielded and mended and abiding in Him.
The sovereignty and goodness of God, my reality.
So long getting here, so much learned to forsake.
This new knowledge now I take,
 My future unknown,
But now I hold His hand.
Have pure motives, trust and obey;
El Shaddai knows the way.

Sunrise

No more anguish.
What have I done?
What can I do?
What's the matter with me?
A dark cloud hovering over me.

Childhood experiences,
Innocence taken,
Poor decisions,
Desires of the flesh.
The light was dim,
Illumination elusive.

Break the chains that hold me back.
Now walk in light.
Live set free.
Around me, all the beauty to see.
Find goodness in the world I have.
There is heaven on this side,
As we look to the Heaven of eternity.

Learn

Seeing is believing.
No, believing is seeing.
Lessons each day are mine to receive.

Elohim, Adonai, Jehovah,
My Savior, my Friend.
Do justly, love mercy,
Walk humbly each day.

Obedience as best I can.
Repentance, forgiveness when I fall short.
This is how to say, "I love You too."
That is all that He asks.

Learn today to pave the way for tomorrow.
For whomever has, more will be given.

Released

I sleep at night.
No more tossing and turning.
The man who loved, then didn't,
Oh, but he does, he just got confused.
No longer a consideration for me.

It's the Son of Man I desire to please.
Do I fall short? I can't count the ways.
No more efforts to please one with a void that can't be filled.
The Son of Man didn't come to condemn, but to save.
The Apostle Paul said it well.
For now we see through a glass dimly,
But one day face to face for eternity.

Can't be bitter; life's lessons aren't easy.
My escapes from reality delayed God's plan.
My life goes on, one day at a time.
Mistakes for sure, but they don't devastate.
Ask forgiveness, stay on the path.
His plan to prosper, not to harm.
His work in me not yet done.
Not done until angels carry me to eternity.

Armed

Each morning the devil lies in wait.
He makes his scheme, forms his plan.
Busy, overwhelmed, listening to the judgment of others.
Thinking my job includes judging others.
Deception is his work.
Discouragement is his tool.

Be armed each day, each hour as needed.
Pick up my tools; I keep them close at hand.
His Word, my prayers, Christian fellowship.

Look, seek, and find Him in circumstances,
The kindness of others,
The blessings of each day.

Parallel Lives

Our lives are numbered birth to death.
He lives here and I do too.
This house is plenty big for two.
His life in anger and discontent.
Mine, at peace, at last some balance.

The arrangement is fine.
The children still mine.
No step moms/grand moms,
Or some younger one.
Our current arrangement excludes all those.

So day to day, life goes on.
Trust in the Father is what it takes.
Without anxiety, without fear,
Contentment stays very near.

Forever

Peace . . . at last.
My companions: anxiety and fear.
Exposed without them?
No.
Given to the Father.
Too late?
No.
Eternity awaits.

Future

As the deer pants for the water so pants my soul for You, O God.

—PSALM 42:11, NKJV

Eyes Open

Pleasures,
Now that I'm free.
Love around me I could not see.
Rain to nourish,
Sunshine for warmth.

Wildlife abounds in my backyard.
Squirrels in the trees,
Rabbits just outside the fence.
The crane lingers at the pond.
Deer graze in the meadows,
Just down the road.
All these wonders now I see.

Advice

God gave each of us a body.
Stop finding fault with it.
That's criticizing God's work.

Eat from the earth; simple is better.
Jesus ate; He even feasted,
But you never saw Him over eating.
Exercise; be a good steward of the body you were given.

Don't grumble.
Show hospitality to others.
Be thankful.
Boast only in the Lord.

Speculate

If you must speculate,
Imagine it as good.
Imagine the profound,
The kind,
The helpful,
The altruistic.
It could happen.
It just might be true.

Forgive

Forgiveness, no choice,
For a Christian, I know.
Many years for me to understand.

God gave His Son.
He atones for my sin.
He has also taken my guilt and shame.

How do I give my love?
My thanks for this love so undeserved,
But so freely given?
I forgive others as I have been forgiven.

Position is important.
It must be in Christ.
Forgiving others frees me to walk in light.
My love shown in obedience and trust.

Not permission for the offender to continue.
Each must find his own way to Him.

Challenging

Trust in the Lord with all your heart and lean not on your own understanding. In all your ways acknowledge Him, and He will direct your paths.

—PROVERBS 3:5–6

Challenging

Have I sounded sublime?
Like I had it together?
I thought I did.
So many positive steps I have taken.

Parallel lives works to a point.
Living like that after so many years,
Requires stamina and a resolve,
I can't seem to summon.
Despite my logic and intentions,
It's leaving me stressed and spent inside.

My courage, my resolve, my faith needs a boost.
Honestly, I need more than a boost.
I need better sleep, better focus for study.
I need some assistance.
But where do I turn?

Harder Than I Thought

Life on this path
Is often stressful.
A pretense for others
Each day maintained.

A peaceful semblance
For family to see.
Not always successful at
Avoiding skirmishes with him.

Where once vodka
Seemed a balm.
I know it was actually
A deceptive calm.
Talking with others,
Giving mutual support,
A strategy for success,
For continued healing.
An addition to my life,
I feel I am needing.

Afterthoughts

I thought I had it,
That I finally understood.
I think I'm good, fit to go on.

But,
Habits are reinforced.
Thoughts hammered in.
Brain retraining is a possibility.
Thoughts fired together, wired together?
Is brain plasticity real?
Can I relearn my thinking?
Can I help myself become new?

Can I be sprinkled with clean water
As the prophet Ezekiel explained?
Can I have that heart of flesh,
With a new spirit?
The Word and power of God live.

Jesus invites us to find rest in Him.
He is gentle and humble in spirit.
His yoke is easy; His burden light.
When I learn from Him,
I find rest for my soul.

Hereafter

Do I think of the hereafter?
You bet I do! I smile.
Many times I go upstairs,
And think, "What am I here after?"
At last, it comes to me.
Although sometimes I have to go downstairs,
And then go back up again.

What about the Great Hereafter?
Revelation lived in front of me.
A different kind of smile you see.
Christians have nothing to fear.
Every day moves us closer.

Not everyone is going.
That's abundantly clear.
There are those who should live in fear.
They think a good person is all that's expected.
Their lust, their lies, their conceit don't matter.
"Life Is Good," is their alma mater.
They think,
"I have this covered.
I'm self sufficient.
Whatever I think and whatever feels good to me.
That's what will get me there."

How?

How can I try to love him?
Must I really try?
His prayers effusive, full of religiosity.
My goal to encourage, give respectability.
Maybe I've erred, didn't give what was due.
Or perhaps I've given more than I should.
How do I balance, keep something for me?

Yet
His pattern to think of his needs and others,
With little thought for me.

Promise

I'm stronger.
He sees it,
Knows that it's true.

In community I have found strength,
A focus to live as I believe.
He still tries to bluff me.
Denial his perpetual first response.

I'm a good student.
I've researched and learned.
Found the trail up to and
Proving my point.

In words less delicate than these,
I tell him how insulted and offended I am.
"You spend time intimately viewing the bodies of others,
Then you expect to be welcomed to mine.
No matter what caveat you add,
It's not acceptable for the man you claim to be."
His answer took me totally by surprise,
"It will never happen again. I promise."
How can I know this?
I can't.

How can I know his promise is kept?
I can't see his mind or look into his heart.
I suspect there is more than he admits.
I can tell volumes by the fruit that he bears, and
I can tell volumes by his attitude toward me.

No Regrets

I always wanted a family of my own.
Without him, I would not have them.

Without him, maybe I would not have learned to forgive.
Without him, maybe I would not have learned to wait on the Lord.
Without him, maybe I would not have learned true empathy with pain.
Without him, maybe I would have held onto old hurts.
Without him, maybe my faith would not have grown.
Maybe I needed time in the wilderness?
I needed time in the wilderness.

I'm still learning to be anxious for nothing.
To trust an unknown future to God whom I know.
To commit and wait for direction.
To live today and not any other.

Even with His help,
There are days that I flounder.

Next

And do not be conformed to this world, but be ye transformed by the renewing of your mind, that you may prove what is that good and acceptable and perfect will of God.

—ROMANS 12:2, NKJV

My Parents

Mother
A child of depression.
Sometimes no meal in sight.
Basically self-educated.
Strong willed and determined.
We learned by her example how to work.
Scarred by her mother's early death.
Her father, widowed, soon remarried.
Widowed again, then married one half his age.
Scarred by her father's neediness.

Father
A child of depression.
Sometimes no meal in sight.
Educated little.
Skilled in his trade, but easily deterred.
Often found reasons not to work.
Looking for income that required little.
Scarred by his mother's doting on her only child.
Scarred by his father's drunken binges.

How did they ever stay together?
At the end, each humble and contrite.
Forgiven, each hobbled in fading light,
Assisted by angels into eternity.

R & R

Repentance and regret, not synonyms.
Regret, "should have" and "if only".
Repentance, sees sin like God does.
Regret, stagnant.
Repentance, fluid.
Regret, paralyzing.
Repentance, freeing.
Regret, discouragement.
Repentance, encouragement.
Regret, the devil's tool.
Repentance, the work of Jesus on the cross for me.

Community

Jesus, Wonderful Counselor,
The Great Physician,
Chose to heal in many ways.
From near, from far,
By Word, by touch.
He even used His spittle.
The winds and seas obey His voice.

So long I diligently worked to be
What I thought God planned for me.
Many times I thought I was healed.
The opposite has been revealed.

Knowing I couldn't continue this way,
I researched, explored, and rejected many.
I finally found His plan for me.
Information, instruction, and inspiration.
Healing would come in community.
These fellow believers who listen to me.
Not like others trying to fix me.
I have always wanted to serve.
The perfect place: as they help me,
I can help them.
What about tomorrow?
I can't say.

But I do know that today
Holds an equanimity that's new to me.
My firm belief that Jesus chose
To heal me in community.

Maturity

Calm in the midst of storm,
Can become a reality.
I haven't arrived, but
I'm making progress.

Able to function and face the storm.
Able to learn from it and help another.
Able to make it a stepping stone.
Seeing the past not as an anchor, but as a rudder.

Today

The best day of my life;
The only day there is.
Yesterday has passed.
There is no tomorrow;
When it arrives, it is today.
When can we change?
When are new habits formed?
When do we bond with friends?
When can we make amends?
When can we make memories?
When can love be expressed?

Today

History

Learn from the past.
Don't live in it.
My past is my personal history.
Hold onto hurts,
And they perpetuate.
Resent those who hurt you,
And they multiply.

It takes diligence and prayer
To keep pride out of my way.
Pray to want what God wants.
Pray to see myself as God sees me.
Pray that I will see others as God does.
Pray for the lost and where
I have been spitefully used.
It is God's will that none will perish.
As Ezekiel saw,
God can bring dry bones to life.

Nothing happens that God does not allow.
His purpose as in these famous lines:
"Bless all the dear children in Thy tender care,
And fit us for Heaven to live with You there." [1]

---

1. Gabriel, Charles Hutchinson, "Away in a Manger". Various tunes, lyric variations, and publishers in the late nineteenth century.

Why So Long?

So long to understand.
So long to comprehend.
Never a doubt about God's love.
His sovereignty unquestioned.
His goodness undenied.

But why all the heartache in my life?
Why all the inability to cope?
Why my need to escape
And not even have to think?
Why the knots in my stomach
And my nerves on edge?
Why so long to come to terms
With the life I was given?

Why so long to find the balance
Between giving to others and
Keeping something for myself?
Between having compassion
And giving too much?

For me it has been a lifelong journey.
Each time I thought I had arrived, I hadn't.
Each time I thought I had learned
Reliance on my Heavenly Father,

Only to fall short and know I hadn't.

When I finally stopped trying to analyze and decipher.
When I finally stopped thinking I had arrived.
When my prayer at last became,
"Help me Father, I can't figure it out."
And waited and did nothing.
And waited and did nothing,
And then He revealed:
All the lessons I have learned are indeed valid.
All the growing and maturing were indeed needed.

Now learn the difference between love and indulgence.
Learn the difference between drawing
A line in the sand and setting boundaries,
For others and for myself too.
Learn the nuances and subtleties,
The slight shifting that calls for my attention.
The attention that means I need to step back,
So the boundaries can be clearly seen.

These comprise the elements of tough love and compassion.
Define the difference between control and influence.
With God's direction, the path though still narrow,
Straightens a bit.
Though not so straight that I can see far ahead.
One day at a time. One day at a time.

Take Heart

Keep doing the same thing,
Expecting a different result:
The definition of insanity.

Be anxious for nothing.
Trust in the Lord.
The past cannot be changed,
Nor can I change others.
Give no audience for poor behavior.
Forsake lamenting what never was.
Jesus loves me.
His grace is sufficient.
Walk with Jesus.
Learn from His life.
Embrace gratitude.
Share the Gospel.
Show hospitality.
Pray about everything;
It doesn't depend on me.
My home is in Heaven.

Take heart.
Jesus has overcome the world.
His strength is made perfect in weakness.

Another Today

When can I become an influence for good?
When can I choose to see blessings throughout the day?
When can I show kindness to a stranger?
When can I be supportive without becoming a crutch?
When can I be thankful for God's patience with me?
When can I find humility and forgive as often as it takes?
When can I begin to understand waiting on the Lord?
When can I realize how much God loves families?
When can I acknowledge that the same God who holds atoms together and put the stars in place has held my family together?
When can I accept that what I thought and hoped was not to be?
When can I know that where I end up is far more important than where I began?
When can I know God, though He did not create it, uses evil for good?
When can I be in awe that He works all things for good for His children?
When can I love more as Jesus loves?
When can Jesus be Lord of my life?

Today

Next

Is there another chapter?
There probably is.
As for my life,
I hope the story has been told.
The days to come lived one by one.
Each day is the one that matters.
Trusting a future I do not know.
To the God that I know.
I knew Him from a very young age.
Always working to be the woman I thought He planned.
Finally getting it; He really is in charge.
Not for each day, but for each moment too.
Finally understanding.
My recent past has been the best.
Today, the only day, is now the best.

Your Neighbor

Do you know the person next to you?
The one on the street passing you?
The one in the neighborhood walking the dog?
The one at the cashier in front of you?
The one in the church pew singing a song?

What struggles, what trials,
They may be going through?
What heartaches, what burdens,
They may carry?

Many requests are shared,
And for these we must pray.
Many unspoken requests and
For these too we must pray.

But what of those carried in solitude?
Too embarrassingly painful to be uttered out loud?
Not said aloud, but only in print.
Not shared as a request, but for encouragement.
The desire that some others might find hope.
See a glimmer that aids perspective.
See an example that supports persevering.
Who prays for her readers but desires anonymity.

Why Leah Johns?

Leah (in *Genesis*)—I feel I may know something of how she felt.

Johns—In all the Bible, John's writing most touches my heart.

Final Thoughts

LIFE IS NOT A COURT of law where every word and action must be examined for the reader to understand the story. Trials and tribulations take many forms. You are not alone, my sisters and my brothers. You may have your own story of challenges or yours might easily fit within these pages. Regardless of where you are in living your story, these words from Isaiah, the prophet, provide hope and encouragement.

> "Come now, and let us reason together," says the Lord.
> "Though your sins are like scarlet,
> They shall be as white as snow;
> Though they are red like crimson,
> They shall be as wool.
> If you are willing and obedient,
> You shall eat the good of the land,
> But if you refuse and rebel,
> You shall be devoured by the sword";
> For the mouth of the Lord has spoken.
> (Isa 1:18–21, NKJV)

On a night that now seems long ago, I could not sleep, though I was exhausted. I questioned God through the night and decided that I must write this story, and then I slept.

These words of poetry began to come to me—at first wisps, hard for me to catch. Each day brought new words; some days there were many words. I had to write them before any more would come. There was no outline, no filling in. One line followed another until the writing was complete. Since then, there have been

Final Thoughts

no more words for me to write—no ideas, no words for thoughts or memories to record.

The writing has given me clarity and a new perspective. I pray another can find the glimmer that leads to the Light Who takes away all darkness. He is always there. Sometimes we have to get in a new position to see Him better.

"Away in a Manger" is one of my favorite songs all through the year. Part of it tells us,

> Away in a manger, no crib for a bed.
> The little Lord Jesus lay down His sweet head.
> The stars in the bright sky looked down where He lay.
> The little Lord Jesus asleep on the hay.
>
> Be near me Lord Jesus, I ask thee to stay,
> Close by me forever and love me I pray.
> Bless all the dear children in Thy tender care,
> And fit us for Heaven to live with You there.[1]

To fit us for Heaven to live with Him: the reason He came from Heaven to Earth, the reason King Jesus left Heaven to be born in a manger, and the reason the Son of God came to walk among us.

God is sovereign.
God is good.
His timing is perfect.
God is merciful.
God gives grace to the humble.
And so we must forgive and wait on the Lord to find the joy of the Lord and our strength.

---

1. Gabriel, Charles Hutchinson.

Bibliography

Gabriel, Charles Hutchinson, "Away in a Manger". Various tunes, lyric variations, and publishers in the late nineteenth century.

"Hush Little Baby". Traditional lullaby thought to have been written in the Southern United States. Author and date of origin are unknown.

www.ingramcontent.com/pod-product-compliance
Lightning Source LLC
Chambersburg PA
CBHW071136090426
42736CB00012B/2135